THE LI

B]

GW00729228

Compiled by
DOMINIC WILLS

CARLTON
BOOKS

THIS IS A CARLTON BOOK

First published in 2003 by
Carlton Books Limited
20 Mortimer Street
London W1T 3JW

ISBN 1 84222 904 4

Printed in Singapore

INTRODUCTION

'We were always waiting to see who was going to be bigger than The Beatles, and it was The Beatles'. So said Paul McCartney, in 1997, when The Beatles' *Anthology 1* album topped the charts. It was to be expected, really. After all, hadn't The Beatles invented the sixties, and Liverpool, and pop music as we know it today? Hadn't they turned the world on to pot, and peace, and ended the war in Vietnam? Weren't they hailed by royalty, presidents and fans the globe over – the biggest pop phenomenon ever?

The following quotes and soundbites tell their story, revealing the working practices, the loves and animosities, the quirky humour and incisive wit, the triumphs and the terrible tragedies of the most influential pop band in history.
And then there's the message, too. Peace.

**The author would like to
acknowledge the following sources:**

Pete Best (Plexus Publishing), Richard Buskin
(Alpha Books), *Daily Mirror*, *Datebook*, Hunter Davies,
London Evening Standard, Geoffrey Giuliano
(Sunburst Books, Smith Gryphon), George Harrison,
Hulton Getty, *LA Times*, Cynthia Lennon, Paul McCartney,
Mojo, Scott Muni (MacDonald), *National Insider*,
New Musical Express, *New York Daily News*,
New York Times, *Newsweek*, The *Observer*, *Playboy*,
Denny Somach et al. (Macdonald), *Rolling Stone*,
RKO Radio, Steve Turner (Carlton Books)

❛We were always pushing ahead; "louder, further, longer, more different". I always wanted things to be different because we knew that people, generally, always want to move on❜.

PAUL explains the band's rampant innovation

‘We [had] a zinc bath, a big one, hanging on the wall outside. We used to bring it in and put it in front of the kitchen fire and then fill it from pans and kettles with hot water’.

GEORGE HARRISON on childhood poverty

6 I was an engineer, working in a factory...
learning how to do blueprints,
bend metal, hammer and chisel.
And I made a conscious decision,
"I am a musician".
And I left the factory 9.

RINGO STARR recalls the bad old days
in *Ticket To Ride*

'Crap. Terrible. Rubbish. John and Paul had talent, but the band was terrible'.

GERRY MARSDEN tells *Ticket To Ride* why the Quarry Men never made it

'[It] came in a vision – a man
appeared on a flaming pie
and said unto them
"From this day on you are
Beatles with an A"'.

JOHN LENNON, from his prose piece 'Being A Short
Diversion on the Dubious Origins of Beatles', 1961

'Nothing really affected
me until Elvis.
Without him there
would be no Beatles'

JOHN remembers the King

'At one point, Liverpool –
maybe it still is – was the capital
of Country & Western music in England...
Johnny Ray was my first real hero,
but that was after Gene Autry,
the singing cowboy.
What a great voice '.

HATS OFF to Ringo

6 I still love Little Richard and I love Jerry Lee Lewis. They're like primitive painters... Chuck Berry is one of the all-time great poets... He was well-advanced for his time, lyric-wise. We all owe him a lot 9.

JOHN, to *Rolling Stone*

‘There was a feeling we all had, built into us all, that something was going to happen. I felt extremely positive. It was just a matter of time and how to get it happening ’.

GEORGE feels the beat on the street

'The Beatles didn't begin in Liverpool, really. The Beatles were born in the streets of Hamburg... The lowlife, the hard life, the club life, the characters, the input, the output. That's what fuses bands together'.

The Animals' **ERIC BURDON** (to *Ticket To Ride*)

> ‘What with the playing, drinking and birds, how could we find time to sleep?’

JOHN, on life in Hamburg

' We shared everything in those days, and for the nightly romp there were usually five or six girls between the four of us '.

PETE BEST, original Beatles drummer, dishes the Hamburg dirt to Geoffrey Giuliano

❝ His contribution to the band was brilliant, regardless of the fact that he didn't have the same musical abilities as the rest of us. He was a powerhouse, simply because of his charisma onstage. He was the guy who looked like James Dean **❞**.

PETE BEST remembers Stuart Sutcliffe, the first fifth Beatle, who died of a brain haemorrhage in 1962

❝I think that Stuart was John's closest and dearest friend... They were on the same wavelength, but they were opposites. Stuart was a sensitive artist and he was not a rebel, as John was**❞**

CYNTHIA LENNON talks to *Ticket to Ride*

❝ I couldn't be bothered with [George] when he first came around. He used to follow me round like a bloody kid... It took me years to come around to him, to start considering him as an equal **❞**.

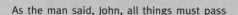

As the man said, John, all things must pass

'More often than not too many people would laugh. It was just stupid. We didn't want to appear as a gang of idiots'.

PAUL MCCARTNEY explains why the boys dumped the all-leather look

‘It was a traumatic experience because we were doing numbers by Ray Charles and Little Richard and it was hard to suddenly start singing "Love Me Do". We thought that our numbers were a bit wet’.

JOHN on early Lennon/McCartney compositions

‘Look, I'm interested in managing you. I've never managed a group before, but I'm prepared to have a go at it’.

BRIAN EPSTEIN'S first words to The Beatles

‘I was immediately struck by their music, their beat and their sense of humour, and even afterwards, when I met them, I was struck again by their personal charm**’**

BRIAN EPSTEIN – one step ahead of the world

' Brian was a beautiful guy...
an intuitive, theatrical guy,
and he knew we had something.
He presented us well **'**.

JOHN recalls Brian's brain

'The Beatles won't go, Mr Epstein.
We know these things.
You have a good record
business in Liverpool.
Why not stick to that?'

DICK ROWE, Head of A&R at Decca,
blows it badly in 1962

‘ Congratulations, boys.
EMI request recording session.
Please rehearse new material ’.

BRIAN EPSTEIN'S telegram to the boys
in Hamburg, 1962

‘ Ringo kept sitting in with the band, and every time Ringo sat in with the band it just felt like this was it ’.

GEORGE sees times a-changin'

Epstein: ❛The boys want you out and Ringo in❜.

Best: ❛Why?❜

Epstein: ❛They don't think you're a good enough drummer, Pete. And George Martin doesn't think you're a good enough drummer❜.

It's the end of the line for Pete Best, August 16, 1962

> 'Never to my face, during my two years as a Beatle, did one of them declare that my drumming was not up to standard... Right to the end we were still drinking together and seemingly the best of friends'.

Pete Best never saw it coming.

> 'Pete forever, Ringo never'.

Fans on the streets of Liverpool.
Fists flew for weeks between rival factions.

6 George had done no rock and roll and we'd never been in the studio, so we did a lot of learning together 9.

JOHN, on first working with George Martin

George Martin: ❝Is there anything that you don't like?❞

George Harrison: ❝Well, I don't like your tie, for a kick-off❞.

Is this how to behave at your first EMI demo session?

'The Beatles are whacky. They wear their hair like a mop – but it's WASHED, it's super-clean. So is their fresh young act. They don't have to rely on off-colour jokes about homos for their fun'

The *Daily Mirror* in 1963, before the days of political correctness

❝I hope to have enough money to go into a business of my own by the time we do flop. It may be next week, it may be two or three years, but I think we'll be in the business... for at least another four years **❞**.

GEORGE – the sensible one

‘For our last number I'd like to ask your help. Would the people in the cheaper seats clap your hands... and the rest of you, if you'll just rattle your jewellery’.

JOHN cheeks the Queen Mother at the 1963 Royal Command Performance

❝If I get stuck on the middle eight
of a new number, I give up,
knowing that when I see John
he will finish it off for me.
He'll bring a new approach to it
and that particular song will finish up
half and half, Lennon and McCartney❞.

PAUL, on the world's
most famous songwriting partnership

'My contribution to Paul's songs was always to add a little bluesy edge to them'.

JOHN clarifies some more

‘ The Presleyan gyrations and caterwauling of yesterday are but lukewarm dandelion tea in comparison to the 100-proof elixir served up by The Beatles ’.

The *New York Daily News*
senses something coming in 1964

"It would not seem quite so likely that the accompanying fever known as Beatlemania will also be successfully exported. On this side of the Atlantic, it is dated stuff"

New York Times critic **JACK GOULD**.
Four weeks later, The Beatles arrived in America...

'The Beatles – they're a passing phase, symptoms of the uncertainty of the times and the confusion around us'.

Evangelist **BILLY GRAHAM**

❛Everybody else thought they were for the teenyboppers, that they were gonna pass right away. But it was obvious to me that they had staying power. I knew they were pointing the direction where music had to go❜.

BOB DYLAN on his great competitors

Reporter: **'** How did you find America? **'**

Ringo: **'** We went to
Greenland and made a left turn **'**.

They don't make interviewees like this anymore

'Anytime you spell Beatle
with an 'a' in it, we get some money'.

RINGO enjoys the lsd
(that's pounds, shillings and pence)

6 When I feel my head start to swell,
I look at Ringo and know
perfectly well we're not supermen 9.

JOHN unsheaths the rapier wit once more

Reporter: **❛**What do you think of Beethoven?**❜**

Ringo: **❛**I love him. Especially his poems**❜**.

Another press conference special

‘We're going to start
a campaign to stamp out Detroit’.

PAUL, when told there's a
Stamp Out The Beatles campaign in Detroit

❝ We never play to segregated
audiences and we're not going to start now.
I'd rather lose our appearance money **❞**.

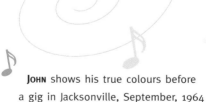

JOHN shows his true colours before
a gig in Jacksonville, September, 1964

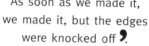

❛What we generated was fantastic, when we played straight rock, and there was nobody to touch us in Britain. As soon as we made it, we made it, but the edges were knocked off**❜**.

JOHN tells *Rolling Stone* the price of fame

'Beatles Bedroom Scandal
Police Find A Sexy Blonde Teen
In Paul's Room'

One *National Insider* headline in 1965

"An average feature film of the time would cost over £1.5 million. I eventually got UA to push the budget for *A Hard Day's Night* up to £180,000. It must be one of the cheapest films ever made".

Producer **DENIS O'DELL** gives the score to *Mojo*

' Help! was a drag because we didn't know what was happening... We were on pot by then and all the best stuff is on the cutting-room floor, with us breaking up and falling all over the place '.

JOHN discusses 1965 recording techniques with *Rolling Stone*

'I can't believe it.
I thought you had to drive tanks
and win wars **'**.

JOHN, on receiving the MBE in 1965

‘She's lovely.
She was very friendly.
She was just like a mum to us’.

PAUL, after receiving the award from the Queen

Reporter: 'What will you do with your medals?'

Paul: 'What you normally do with medals. Put them in a box'.

Well, ask a silly question...

'The British house of royalty has put me on the same level as a bunch of vulgar numbskulls'.

Canadian MP **HECTOR DUPUIS**
– not so happy with his MBE

'Your Majesty, I am returning this MBE in protest against Britain's involvement in the Nigeria–Biafra thing, against our support of America in Vietnam, and against "Cold Turkey" slipping down the charts. With love, John Lennon of Bag'

JOHN'S letter to the Queen, 1969

‘It was originally called... "Scrambled Eggs".
It fits: "Scrambled eggs, oh my baby
how I love your legs". You know,
if you don't have any lyrics yet
and you want to play someone a song,
you have to kind of say something ’.

PAUL explains the humble origins
of 'Yesterday' to Scott Muni

❛It flipped me out so much that I determined to try the same thing – to make an entire album that was a gas❜.

Rubber Soul inspires Beach Boy **BRIAN WILSON** to make *Pet Sounds*

> '''Christianity will go.
> It will vanish and shrink.
> I needn't argue about that;
> I'm right and I will be proved right.
> We're more popular than Jesus now'''.

JOHN, to the *Evening Standard*, 1966

‘We're bigger than Jesus’.

Datebook magazine misquotes John,
sparking threats from the KKK and bonfires
of Beatles merchandise across the US

‘You know, I’m not saying that we’re better or greater, or comparing us with Jesus Christ as a person, or God as a thing, or whatever it is. I just said what I said and it was wrong, or was taken wrong, and now it’s all this...’

JOHN apologises, kind of

❛I'd actually stopped trying to think of something. Nothing would come. I was cheesed off and went for a lie-down, having given up. Then I thought of myself as Nowhere Man – sitting in his nowhere land❜.

JOHN finds his muse between the sheets [to Hunter Davies]

❛ I knew 'Yellow Submarine' would get connotations, but it really was a children's song **❜**.

PAUL explodes that drug-anthem myth, but Nembutal capsules still became known as yellow submarines

❝I reckon we could send out
four waxwork dummies of ourselves
and that would satisfy the crowds.
Beatles concerts are nothing
to do with music any more**❞**.

JOHN bemoans the effect of Beatlemania

‘The seed was planted when The Beatles stopped touring and I couldn't deal with not being onstage. But I was too frightened to step out of the palace.’

JOHN tells *Newsweek* when the band's problems began

6 I've always needed a drug to survive.
Of course, the others did too,
but I was always the worst.
I wanted more of everything, because
I'm probably crazier than the rest 9

JOHN, always curious, always hungry

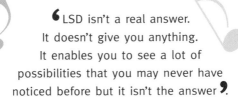

' LSD isn't a real answer.
It doesn't give you anything.
It enables you to see a lot of
possibilities that you may never have
noticed before but it isn't the answer **'**.

GEORGE gives the score on the doors of perception

‘Sometimes I had songs that were better than some of their songs and we'd have to record maybe eight of theirs before they'd LISTEN to one of mine’.

Don't worry, **GEORGE**, here comes the sun

❝I think "Penny Lane" was Paul's answer to John when he wrote "Strawberry Fields" because he was knocked out by it. He thought it was a marvellous song, and tried to do something better❞.

GEORGE MARTIN explains that competitive vibe to Scott Muni

‘They were growing up and they were like plants in a hot-house... They were thirsty for knowledge, curious to find out what else they could have, and with their fame came the opportunity to experiment ’.

GEORGE MARTIN on the band's rampant innovation

‘We had been told that
we'd be seen recording it by
the whole world at the same time.
So we had one message for the world – love.
We need more love in the world’.

PAUL recalls the band recording ‘All You Need
Is Love’ on the BBC's first ever live global TV link
(to 26 countries) on June 25, 1967

‘People made the mistake of thinking it must be Lennon's because he was so hip. Actually, he was taking so many drugs and trying to get rid of his ego that it was much more McCartney's idea’

Beatles friend **BARRY MILES** explains *Sgt Pepper* to Steve Turner

6 This was the only one on [Sgt Pepper] written as a deliberate provocation. But what we want to do is to turn you on to the truth rather than on to pot **9**.

PAUL on the controversial 'A Day In The Life'

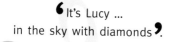

'It's Lucy ...
in the sky with diamonds**'**.

Four-year-old **JULIAN LENNON** explains a painting
he's done. The subject is classmate Lucy O'Donnell

'I knew Lennon quite well.
He used to talk a lot about comedy.
He was a *Goon Show* freak.
It all stopped when he married Yoko Ono.
Everything stopped.
He never asked for me again **'**

SPIKE MILLIGAN, friend of George Martin,
who sat in on some *Sgt Pepper* sessions

‘We were just outside the
lecture hall in Bangor when we heard...
One of the press walked up to us
and said "Brian's dead".
I was absolutely stunned’.

JOHN recalls their manager's untimely death.
The band were attending a
transcendental meditation course

❛I knew we were in trouble then. I didn't really have any misconceptions about our ability to do anything other than play music, and I was scared. I thought "We've f***ing had it"**❜**.

JOHN tells *Rolling Stone* his reaction to Brian Epstein's death

' We went out to make a film and nobody had the vaguest idea of what it was all about. What we should have been filming, if anything, was all the confusion, because that was the REAL mystery tour **'**.

Beatles' assistant **NEIL ASPINALL** on the *Magical Mystery Tour* movie

'Critics And Viewers Boo:
Beatles Produce First Flop With Yule Film'.

THE LA TIMES on the premier of *Magical Mystery Tour*

Hippy: **❝**You are our leader, George.
You know where it's at**❞**.

George: **❝**It's you who should
be leading yourself.
You don't want to be following leaders –
me or anyone else**❞**.

San Francisco, 1967

❛[We're] in the happy position
of not really needing any more money,
so for the first time the bosses
aren't in it for the profit **❜**.

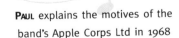

PAUL explains the motives of the
band's Apple Corps Ltd in 1968

> **'**If you come to me and say "I've had such-and-such a dream", I will say "Here's so much money. Go away and do it"**'**.

JOHN, the idealist heart of Apple

❝I sincerely believe in love and peace. I am a violent man who has learned not to be violent and regrets his violence**❞**.

JOHN catches the sixties' spirit

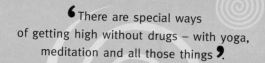

‘There are special ways
of getting high without drugs — with yoga,
meditation and all those things’.

GEORGE sees the light

'John and George were in their element. They threw themselves totally into the Maharishi's teachings, were happy, relaxed, and above all had found a peace of mind that had been denied them for so long'

CYNTHIA LENNON explains the power of the Maharishi Mahesh Yogi

❛John was so funny and so direct that to break the silence he went up to the Maharishi, who was sitting cross-legged on the floor, patted him on the head and said "There's a good guru"❜.

DONOVAN recalls John's humour

❝Well, if you're so cosmic,
you'll know why❞.

JOHN, when the Maharishi asked why the band
were leaving his course in Rishikesh, India.

❝We made a mistake.
We thought there was more
to him than there was. He's human.
We thought at first that he wasn't **❞**

PAUL'S disappointed by the Maharishi

❛It was obvious that ["Revolution"] was a response to people making demands on [John] concerning his radical point of view, and you realized that by our adulation of the group we were making it all the more difficult for them to continue❜.

JAMES TAYLOR, one of the first Apple signings

‘Count me out if it's for violence. Don't expect me on the barricades unless it's with flowers’.

JOHN, on 'Revolution' and revolution

❝I know it sounds corny but we still love each other, but it hasn't worked out. Perhaps we'll be childhood sweethearts and meet again, and get married when we're about 70**❞**

JANE ASHER on her split from Paul in 1968. One month earlier, he'd met one Linda Eastman

❝ Of course I'm a coward.
I wasn't going to go off
and leave Cynthia and be by myself **❞**.

JOHN discusses his marriage break-up

'It was midnight when we started "Two Virgins", it was dawn when we finished, and then we made love at dawn. It was very beautiful'

JOHN describes his first major recording session with Yoko

❛In England they think
I'm someone who has won the pools
and gone off with a Japanese princess.
In America, they treat her with respect.
They treat her as the serious artist she is**❜**.

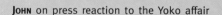

JOHN on press reaction to the Yoko affair

❛[It will] surely see the last vestiges of cultural snobbery and bourgeois prejudice swept away in a deluge of joyful music-making, which only the ignorant will not hear and only the deaf will not acknowledge❜.

Phew! The *Observer*'s **TONY PALMER** reviews *The White Album*.

❚I had a dream about my mother. She had died when I was 14, so I hadn't heard from her in quite a while and it was very good. It gave me some strength. "In my darkest hour, mother Mary comes to me"❛.

PAUL, on the writing of 'Let It Be'

'It's all over now.
It's the end in a way, isn't it?**'**

15-year-old **DIANE ROBBINS** on March 12, 1969,
when Paul married Linda Eastman

‘*Abbey Road* was really unfinished songs all stuck together. Everybody praises the album so much, but none of the songs had anything to do with each other, no thread at all’

JOHN spills the beans to *Playboy*

6 "Maxwell's Silver Hammer" epitomizes the downfalls of life. Just when everything is going smoothly – bang, bang – down comes Maxwell's silver hammer and ruins everything 9.

PAUL on the *Abbey Road* classic

'To get a peaceful life I always let Paul have his own way, even if it meant my songs weren't recorded. But I was having to record Paul's songs, and put up with him telling me how to play my own guitar.'

GEORGE – the man was a saint

❛Do I look dead? I'm fit as a fiddle❜.

Paul to reporter Hugh Farmer in 1969,
when rumours abound that he died in a car crash
in 1966 and was replaced by a lookalike

'One has to completely humiliate oneself to be what The Beatles were... it just happened gradually, bit by bit, until you're doing exactly what you don't want to do with people you simply can't stand '.

JOHN looks back in anger

' We say that peace can only be achieved through peaceful methods, and to fight the establishment with their own weapons is no good, because they've been winning for thousands of years **'**.

JOHN explains his Bed-In in Amsterdam, 1969

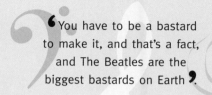

'You have to be a bastard to make it, and that's a fact, and The Beatles are the biggest bastards on Earth'.

JOHN self-deprecates wildly in *Rolling Stone*, 1970

‘Your own space, man, it's so important. That's why we were doomed, because we didn't have any. It's like monkeys in a zoo. They die. You know, everything needs to be left alone’.

GEORGE explains the band's final split

❝I was always waiting for a reason to get out of The Beatles from the day [in 1966] I filmed How I Won The War. I just didn't have the guts to do it❞.

JOHN tells *Newsweek* the split was a long time coming

❝I was cursing because
I hadn't done it.
I wanted to do it,
I should have done it**❞**.

JOHN'S peeved when Paul leaves the band
and makes headlines worldwide

'If the new Beatles soundtrack album *Let It Be* is to be their last, then it will stand as a cheapskate epitaph, a cardboard tombstone, a sad and tatty end to a musical fusion which wiped clean and drew again the face of pop music'

Ouch. **ALAN SMITH** in *NME*, 1970

‘Paul behaved like a spoilt child’.

RINGO, under oath in the High Court in 1971,
as the band's partnership is dissolving

'I was amazed.
I was the biggest Beatle
for two weeks**'**.

RINGO discusses his 1973 solo success
(in *Ticket To Ride*)

> **'**Ringo is just Ringo,
> that's all there is to it.
> And he's every bloody bit as
> warm, unassuming, funny
> and kind as he seems...
> He was quite simply
> the heart of The Beatles**'**.

JOHN knows a Starr when he sees one

‘ Please don't shoot him!
He's a Beatle! ’

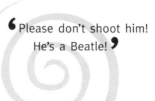

LINDA MCCARTNEY, when she and Paul are held up
by armed muggers in Lagos, 1973

❛I really don't think The Beatles were all that good, you know. I mean, they were fine... fine...**❜**

GEORGE, in 1974. Always the odd one out.

‘The Beatles saved the world from boredom’.

That's more like it, GEORGE

'It seems as if I've been under contract to produce a hit record, artsy book or some daft film since I was about 15, and now I'm tired... I quit. Let someone else carry it on from here'.

JOHN takes time out after Sean is born, 1975

'That man who offered us $5 million each was supposed to also promote a match between a man and a shark, so my suggestion was that he fight the shark and the winner could promote the Beatles concert'

GEORGE, on Bill Sargent's 1976 attempt to reunite the band for one gig

❝ You hear lots of McCartney-influenced
songs on the radio now.
These stories about boring
people doing boring things;
being postmen and secretaries
and writing home... I like to write
about me, 'cause I KNOW me ❞.

JOHN compares his and Paul's work (in *Playboy*)

6 He was pretty rude about me sometimes, but I secretly admired him for it and I always managed to stay in touch with him... I really loved the guy 9.

PAUL, after John's death in December, 1980

'We have lost a genius of the spirit'.

NORMAN MAILER pays his own tribute to John

'Now Daddy is part of God. I guess when you die you become bigger, a part of everything'.

Son **SEAN** learned his lessons well

'As far as I'm concerned, he ranks up there with Kennedy, Martin Luther King and Gandhi as a figure of peace in the world**'**.

DONOVAN on his old friend John

'In the sixties, John Lennon and The Beatles captured the imagination of the entire world. In the songs he composed he leaves behind an extraordinary and permanent legacy'.

President **JIMMY CARTER** speaks for the world

❛We were always waiting to see who was going to be bigger than The Beatles, and it was The Beatles❜.

PAUL, on the outrageous success of *Anthology 1*, 1997

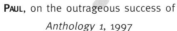

> **"** I had a little throat cancer.
> I had a piece of my
> lung removed in 1997.
> And then I was almost murdered.
> But I seem to feel stronger... **"**

A seemingly unstoppable **GEORGE**

6 He left this world as he
lived in it, conscious of God,
fearless of death, and at peace **9**.

The family statement after
George died of cancer, December, 2001

'He enabled us to make
Life of Brian and other films like
A Private Function – none of these would
have happened without his enthusiasm'

Monty Python's **MICHAEL PALIN** explains
the influence of George's Handmade Films

6[The Beatles] opened up the door for all writing groups and it gave them hope... If it hadn't been for The Beatles, there wouldn't be anyone like us around, the sort of band where there are musician-writers 9.

Led Zeppelin's **JIMMY PAGE** gives due respect (in *Ticket To Ride*)

'What The Beatles were all about was just simple love – 'I Wanna Hold Your Hand', that's the entire gist of it! It's a beautiful thing, and no wonder they were so popular'.

YOKO ONO sums it up to Geoffrey Giuliano

6 Go out there and get peace.
Think peace.
Live peace and breathe peace.
You'll get it as soon as you like 9.

JOHN LENNON